People who have helped the world

LOUIS BRAILLE

by Beverley Birch

OTHER TITLES IN THE SERIES

Marie Curie by Beverley Birch (1-85015-092-3)
The Dalai Lama by Christopher Gibb (1-85015-141-5)
Father Damien by Pam Brown (1-85015-084-2)
Henry Dunant by Pam Brown (1-85015-106-7)
Mahatma Gandhi by Michael Nicholson (1-85015-091-5)
Bob Geldof by Charlotte Gray (1-85015-085-0)
Martin Luther King by Valerie Schloredt and Pam Brown
    (1-85015-086-9)
Florence Nightingale by Pam Brown (1-85015-117-2)
Louis Pasteur by Beverley Birch (1-85015-140-7)
Albert Schweitzer by James Bentley (1-85015-114-8)
Sir Peter Scott by Julia Courtney (1-85015-108-3)
Mother Teresa by Charlotte Gray (1-85015-093-1)
Desmond Tutu by David Winner (1-85015-087-7)
Lech Walesa by Mary Craig (1-85015-107-5)
Raoul Wallenberg by Michael Nicholson and
    David Winner (1-85015-109-1)
Coming Soon
Robert Baden Powell by Julia Courtney (1-85015-180-6)
Charlie Chaplin by Pam Brown (1-85015-143-1)
Maria Montessori by Michael Pollard (1-85015-156-3)

Published in Great Britain in 1990 by
Exley Publications Ltd
16 Chalk Hill, Watford, Herts WD1 4BN, United Kingdom.

British Library Cataloguing in Publication Data
Birch, Beverley.
Louis Braille. — (People who have helped the world).
1. France. Blind persons: Braille, Louis. –
Biographies – For children.
I. Title.
II. Series.
362.4'1'0924

ISBN 1-85015-139-3

Series conceived and edited by Helen Exley.
Picture research: Karen Gunnell.
Research: Diana Briscoe.
Editorial: Margaret Montgomery.

Printed and bound in Hungary.

LOUIS BRAILLE

The blind French boy whose invention has
helped millions of blind people to read

Beverley Birch

EXLEY

Louis' quest

No sound could be heard in the darkness except the deep, regular breathing of sleeping boys, the creak of a rusty iron bedstead, the occasional rustle of bedclothes, and, if you listened carefully, a faint, muffled knocking.

One boy was not asleep. He was sitting up, bedclothes hunched about him against the damp chill of the night, intent on something balanced across his knees. It was a small board, covered with paper, and he was pressing down on it – a short, punching movement of his hand, a pause, then another string of sharp downward punches.

He was not at all troubled by working in the darkness. Nor should he be, for darkness or light made no difference to him. He could not see it. Nor could he see the sleeping boys around him, nor the beds, the windows nor the door. Nor, for that matter, could he see the board he held steadily on his knees, nor the quick movements of his hand.

He was blind. He had been blind for as long as he could remember. His companions in that dark room, all those quietly sleeping boys in their narrow bedsteads on either side, were also blind. But while they slept, he was almost dropping with fatigue, and it would be many hours before he allowed himself the luxury of sleep. His task was not yet done, and there weren't enough hours in the day for him to finish it. On he went, steadily punching the pointed instrument which he held, downward against the board and paper, listening to that muffled knocking sound which the movement made.

This was not the first time fourteen-year-old Louis Braille had spent the hours of the night

In the years 1822 to 1824 in Paris, an invention of world-wide importance took place amidst the dank streets and looming buildings of an area like the one shown here. Official reports of the time tell of the "putrid emanations" and swampy dampness of the place where the world's first school for the blind was sited, in the Latin Quarter of Paris. Here, in a building barred from sunlight, the air thick with the stench of disease, poverty and river mud from the nearby Seine, a blind boy of thirteen began to develop a method of writing and reading for blind people like himself. His system is now the international alphabet of the blind, named after him as braille.

A	B	C	D
E	F	G	H
I	J	K	L
M	N	O	P
Q	R	S	T
U	V	W	X
Y	Z		
and	for	of	the

Louis Braille's alphabet: being blind himself, Louis understood that what blind people lost by having no eyesight, they could regain by using their powerful sense of touch. His alphabet used six dots, raised above the surface of the paper so that they could be felt by the fingers as bumps. With these six dots, he found a way to form all letters, numbers, accents, punctuation, and mathematical signs. The six-dot group was perfectly designed to be felt by a single finger-tip: it could be recognized instantly by a braille reader in the way a sighted reader recognizes the shape of an ordinary letter.

hunched over his board and paper ... and if this wasn't enough, he'd get up early to do some more before the day began, before lessons ate into his free time.

He'd been working at this task for months. He'd even taken it away on holiday to his home, and sat through the long summer on a sunny bank or the farmhouse steps, while his family simply smiled and villagers passed by and nodded to one another, "Ah, there's young Louis at his pin-pricks again!"

Pin-pricks on a piece of paper were all they were to those around Louis. They watched his obsession with amusement and affection, for, when all was said and done, what could a blind boy be doing so seriously that was of much importance? And they shook their heads at his misfortune, wishing him and his game well.

Pin-pricks they were: but pin-pricks destined to become the international alphabet of the blind, the key to the door of literacy, knowledge, learning, culture, for blind people the world over. Once opened, that door could never again be slammed closed against them, locking them in a darkness of sightlessness made a thousand times worse by their enforced ignorance.

Within sixty years, the pin-pricks of fourteen-year-old Louis Braille would be acknowledged internationally as one of the world's greatest gifts from one person to his fellows.

A determined child

Little did Louis Braille in that damp dormitory in Paris in 1823 foresee the vastness of his achievement. He knew only that some way *must* be found for blind people like him and his friends to read books easily – as easily as sighted people do, for blind people to write – as sighted people do, for blind people to share the world's knowledge and take part in making that culture even richer.

And he knew also that a way *could* be found. It was a conviction born of his own passionate desire for learning. It was born also of his youth and energy, which would not allow him to be discouraged, of hope, that the tragedy of blindness did not

Braille: using just six dots, like a domino, sixty-three combinations could be formed, to give a complete system for writing and reading: for example, to make the first ten letters of the alphabet (a – j), the top two rows of dots are used; for the next ten letters (k – t) one more dot, from the third row, is added. So **a** is formed by dot 1, and **b** by dots 1 and 2; **k** is then made by dots 1 and 3 (**a** with dot 3 added); **l** by dots 1, 2, and 3 (**b** with dot 3 added.

have to be compounded by the misery of a life hemmed in by ignorance and dependence on others, cut off from the life of society by a thousand barriers.

It *was possible* to find a way. Louis knew it. He would not rest until he found it.

The saddler's son from Coupvray

Louis Braille had not always been blind. For the first three years of his life he had his sight, and had filled the family house with the explorations and curiosity of any young child surrounded by the love and attention of his family. He gave great amusement to his brother and sisters: Louis-Simon, at

"Access to communication in the widest sense is access to knowledge, and that is vitally important for us if we are not to go on being despised or patronized by condescending sighted people. We do not need ptiy, nor do we need to be reminded that we are vulnerable. We must be treated as equals – and communication is the way we can bring this about."
Louis Braille.

seventeen already feeling himself a young man, nineteen-year-old Catherine-Joséphine, and fourteen-year-old Marie-Céline. This baby of the family, young Louis, was so full of energy and curiosity about his small world, such a bundle of cheerful chatter and eager questions!

Louis brought a particular glow of warmth to his mother and father, for he had come into their lives late, when his mother, Monique, was already forty-one and his father, Simon-René, forty-four. At Louis' birth, Simon-René had declared proudly that the boy would be the support and the companion of his old age.

A country village in France, typical of the time. Louis' village, Coupvray, had a weekly market day which attracted people from many nearby villages; each year there were four fairs for the villagers to enjoy, and the main event of the year, the grape harvest. The rhythm of the countryside controlled village life – the planting and care of the crops, the success or failure of the harvests. Louis' father, the local saddler and harness-maker, provided an important skill in these days of horse-drawn farm machinery and transport.

A country childhood

Louis was born on January 4, 1809, in the village of Coupvray, about forty kilometres east of Paris and close to the great, wide, flat expanse of the wheat-growing lands of La Brie. Nestling on the slopes of gentle, wooded hills above the valleys of the River Marne, Coupvray was a bustling, rural village. It boasted a tailor, a ropemaker, a weaver, a locksmith, a doctor, a chemist and a midwife. But its people were mainly farmers and vine-growers and craftspeople whose skills were vital to a farming community: a blacksmith, a wheelwright, and Louis' father, Simon-René, the village saddler and

9

harness-maker. His was a highly-skilled trade much in demand in these days of horse-drawn transport; Simon-René's father had followed the trade before him, and Simon-René hoped both his sons would do the same.

It was a simple, ordinary, busy life: the family owned the farmhouse and Simon-René's workshop, as well as seven-and-a-half acres of land and vineyards in the village, a cow and poultry. It kept them fully occupied and provided a reasonable supply of food throughout the year. They were not rich, but neither did they want for the essentials of life, nor for good friends in their hard-working, tightly-knit community. A weekly market day drew in people from other villages; there were also four fairs each year, and the pinnacle of the year, the grape harvest and its celebrations.

The family house stood in the Chemin des Buttes, but in recognition of the inventor who spent his early childhood there, the road was later renamed Rue Louis Braille. Here Louis would play or chatter to his mother as she went about her work in the stone farmhouse which squatted sturdily below its huge roof, with its dark, leaded windows, massive oak doors and vast chimney. When Louis grew bored, he could visit his father in the workshop across the yard.

What a place of fascination this was! This room was full of bridles, reins and straps, rich with the smell of oiled leather, its corners occupied by the heavy cone-shaped wood-blocks for the horses' collars. And in the middle of it all, the sturdy bench over which his father leaned to do his cutting and shaping of leather. There was an array of shining tools – knives for cutting the leather, and awls for making holes, all polished and razor sharp.

We do not know the exact story of how Louis Braille was blinded, nor which tool plunged into his eye. Some reports say it was a saddler's knife; others that it was an awl, a tool for making holes. Louis himself, in later life, only remembered that it was a sharp, pointed instrument. This painting by A. Harfort shows him reaching for a saddler's knife. The painting now hangs in his father's workshop in Coupvray, where the Braille family home is preserved as a museum.

The plunge into darkness

There are no written records of the blinding of Louis Braille. Nor of exactly when it took place, in that year of 1812. The story has been drawn together from different people's memories; the rest we have to imagine for ourselves. But it is not difficult to picture the curious three-year-old, intent

Above: The workshop and saddler's tools belonging to Louis' father, Simon-René Braille. This is where Louis was blinded.

Right: The cellar stairs in Louis' home. When the accident happened, Louis was an energetic three-year-old with confidence about his world – his home, the village streets, the villagers he saw every day.

As his eyesight faded, he lost everything that was familiar. He could no longer use shape, lighting or size to recognize the things he knew. Day and night were the same and everything dissolved into a formless muddle of sounds and smells he could not recognize. He faced a struggle to re-learn everything: to climb stairs and go through doors he could not see, find his way around furniture, dress and eat, to replace the <u>look</u> of things with their feel, smell, sound and taste. In time, all memory of colours faded.

on copying the exciting tasks he saw his father doing daily, climbing on to the high wood bench, perhaps when Simon-René was outside for a moment in the yard talking to a farmer about repairs needed to some harness.

One can imagine Louis seizing a piece of leather, reaching for a knife, eagerly imitating those precise, intricate movements of his father's skilled hands.

But in the chubby hands of a three-year-old, the sharp cutting instrument of craft and skill was merely a crude, all-too-efficient instrument of destruction. We know of a scream from the workshop, the sobbing boy found with blood pouring down his face. It seems that the clumsily-wielded tool had slipped and sliced into his eye.

His panic-stricken parents did all they could; fresh water and white linen to bandage the bleeding eye. An old woman of the village who understood the healing properties of herbs brought lily-water and they put a dressing on the eye.

"In those days blind people were treated as a useless burden, as lunatics were at that time. Their parents often resented them, even grudging them their keep. Many poor parents sent their children to a workhouse, or sold them as freaks to a fun fair – or, worse, turned them out into the streets to fend for themselves."
Norman Wymer, from "The Inventors".

Permanent blindness

Louis stopped crying, the blood stopped flowing, and the local doctor was at once consulted. But in those days, doctors did not understand the causes and control of infection; it was long before the work of the scientist Louis Pasteur taught them about germs and how infection develops and is carried – on hands, bandages, in the air. It was more than a hundred years before Alexander Fleming discovered penicillin, the first antibiotic which could cure infections by killing dangerous germs without harming the patient.

Helplessly, doctors and family alike watched Louis' injured eye become red and puffy; the eyelid swelled, and looked bruised. Whatever infection had taken hold now spread to the other eye. Objects around him became blurred, as though he was looking at them through a mist. One can imagine him becoming more clumsy and more cautious. The family slowly adjusted to his bumpings and crashings as he collided with furniture, missed his footing on the steps, or dropped his plate as he reached to put it on the table. These were the symptoms of a

13

creeping darkness that, by the time he was five, had descended permanently over Louis.

We are told of visits to an eye doctor in the nearby town of Meaux, but everything was useless. Nothing could be done to save the eyesight of Louis Braille. He would never see, from either eye, again.

Louis adapts

Gradually, Louis must have changed: sighted children learn to imitate – by expression of eyes, mouth, tilt of head and hand gestures – the actions of those around them. But these memories would slowly have receded from Louis' mind, his face growing quieter, more withdrawn, his head taking on the slight forward and sideways tilt, we are told that he carried throughout his life.

His whole body focused now on surviving without being able to see, replacing his sight with his

To Louis' parents, his future must have seemed a hopeless one. How could a blind person earn a living? As long as they were alive, they could care for him. But what then? Most blind people depended on others to give them charity, for they could not earn a living. Many were beggars on the streets. A few, like those in this picture, might hope for a few coins for playing music.

other senses. He began to recognize the sound of his footsteps on different surfaces, the varying echoes of his voice as it bounced off walls, doors, furniture. He learned to recognize the noises of the street outside, the rumble of cartwheels, the jingle of his father carrying harnesses, the murmurs of people's voices, the barking of dogs, filling his world with the sounds and feel of things he could no longer see.

And we can imagine the busy household finding tasks for Louis to do because they found that he had an amazing ability to tell what things were by just touching them, as if his fingers had already replaced the lost eyes. He was able to sort shapes and thicknesses of leather for his father, and later make fringes for the harness. He could sort vegetables and eggs for his mother and sisters as they rushed to prepare for the weekly market.

Gradually Louis forgot what it had ever been like to see; he became a little more adventurous in the world of darkness he now inhabited, more adept at knowing exactly *which* dog had barked, *whose* cart-wheels had rolled up to his father's workshop, *who* had called to him cheerily. He no longer bumped and crashed around the house, for now he knew it by sound as well as touch.

An occupied country

It was not to last long, this unbroken pattern of life in Coupvray. In early 1814, the citizens of Coupvray were shaken by the news that France's army, led by Emperor Napoleon, had been defeated by the combined forces of the Austrians, Russians and Prussians the previous October and was now in full retreat. The troops were short of food and falling back in disorder to the capital, Paris.

The official records of Coupvray tell us something of the progress of Napoleon's retreat and the enemy army's advance across France: January 2, 1814, Coupvray was instructed to provide 275 bushels of oats for the retreating Napoleonic troops; January 23, it was asked for 132 more bushels; January 28, the order was for 1200 bundles of hay and eight cows; February 8, the baker had to make

The best that Louis Braille might hope for at the time was to learn some simple craft like the basket weaving being done by the blind boy in this picture. Louis had already shown his skill with his fingers, when he helped his father sorting leather in the workshop.

706 loaves of bread for the army; February 20, Napoleon took possession of all the horses and mares of the district, then a dozen cows.

By April, the people of Coupvray had their own evidence of the defeat of Napoleon. He was forced to abdicate and had already been replaced by King Louis XVIII. On April 14, Russian troops, soldiers of the Imperial Russian Army, entered Coupvray, and a series of demands began: food, horses, cows, hay, oats, wagons, for the soldiers of the occupation army.

The Braille household, among many others in Coupvray and elsewhere, had enemy Prussian troops billeted upon them. Now Louis' life echoed to the brusque voices of strangers, new footsteps he had to learn to recognize; his father's workshop bustled with foreign cavalrymen bringing in harness for repair. And always, there was the hushed talk of events he could not fully understand, but which kept the conversation of the grown-ups around him serious and worried, punctuated by those sudden silences when a Prussian soldier came within hearing range.

Russians, Prussians, Bavarians, more Russians. Over the two-year occupation Louis' family had sixty-four different soldiers staying in their house. Louis was seven before the last of them left, in the summer of 1816. Now the citizens of Coupvray could take up the threads of normal life again, try to repair the fabric of their community and recover from the hardship of the occupation years.

A friend

Louis' sixth year, his third year of blindness, was the start of a new era for him. It was the year in which a new parish priest came to Coupvray.

The first task of the Abbé Jacques Palluy was to visit the families of his parish. He soon got to know Louis, and within weeks, priest and child had settled into a pattern of easy friendship and companionship. Seated in good weather in the garden, or in colder weather in the priest's house, the Abbé Palluy undertook a series of lessons with Louis. He told bible stories, taught the blind child to recognize the perfumes and the touch of flowers and to know the sounds of different birds and animals. He talked to him about the seasons of the year and the changing pattern of the day.

Louis listened with fascination and excitement: he began to recognize the smells and birdsongs of the dawn and to feel the creeping cool of the evening before it arrived.

And as the friendship grew, the Abbé Palluy also awakened in Louis a deep religious faith which was to remain with him for the rest of his life.

Louis starts school

Louis reached school age. At the village school there was by now another newcomer to Coupvray, a young, dedicated and enthusiastic schoolmaster, Antoine Bécheret.

Opposite, top: These were years when the turbulence of war reached far and wide across Europe, as other nations struggled for power against the army of Napoleon Bonaparte, Emperor of the French. Defeated at the Battle of Leipzig in October 1813, Napoleon retreated toward Paris, seizing supplies from villages like Coupvray. In the early months of 1814 Coupvray rang to the news of battles just up the road, to the east and south. Then came news of Napoleon's abdication. This picture shows the French in retreat after Napoleon's brief return to power a year later and his final defeat by the British at Waterloo in June 1815.

Opposite, bottom: The countryside of Coupvray. Louis' friendship with the priest, Abbé Palluy, was the turning point in his life. Daily they walked and talked together in the surrounding countryside, while the priest taught Louis to recognize the touch and scent of plants. He saw the mind of his young pupil reaching out continually for more knowledge, and he made up his mind to do all he could to offer this blind six-year-old a better future than a life of dependency, hemmed in by lack of education.

Because most blind people were helpless and uneducated, sighted people had for centuries seen their blindness and clumsiness as a form of stupidity, or something to be laughed at – like clowns. This painting by Brueghel, showing the blind leading the blind, shows the kind of caricature made on the subject. During Louis' childhood, most people's attitudes to the blind were at best thoughtless, and at worst very cruel. The Abbé Palluy was very unusual in his belief in Louis' ability to learn.

No sooner was Bécheret installed, than Abbé Palluy went to see him about Louis. Never mind that most people would say there was no point in giving a blind boy lessons like other children! Never mind that a blind boy could not read or write! A boy like Louis, alert, intelligent, interested in everything around him, must surely benefit from being able to listen to the lessons, from sharing the school life of the other children of the village!

Bécheret agreed: new to his profession, he had no convictions about the pointlessness of teaching a blind child; nor did he have fears about attracting the disapproval of the school authorities for giving a place to someone they would see as an unlikely candidate for education or training of any kind.

So it was that Louis could set off each day, with one of his friends, for the village school. Sitting on his bench in the front, close to the teacher where he could hear every word, Louis drank in the lessons as though he could not learn enough. He seemed to understand and memorize what was said instantly. He seemed never to forget what he had

heard, almost as though the events of history, the places and peoples of geography, opened up a world of the imagination for him to take the place of the world of sight that he had lost.

From the beginning he was at the head of his class, and even at this early stage, he had that determination not to accept that his blindness must be a prison without books, a world without the chance to communicate with his friends, record his thoughts or write his notes. A friend of the Brailles recalled that Louis' father hammered nails into wood in the shape of the letters of the alphabet, and that Louis taught himself to recognize them by touch. There are other stories that his father cut letter-shapes out of leather.

What future for Louis?

But dreams in the head of young Louis were one thing. The real prospects for his future were quite another. There was little hope for blind people in those days. They could not study as sighted people

Above: A school very like the one in Coupvray which Louis attended. Blind children seldom attended school, but Louis was soon coming top of his class.

"Homeless blind people of all ages roamed the streets of most large towns, and even well-educated men and women seemed to find it amusing to watch them groping their way and bumping into buildings. They would throw things at them or trip them up, and then burst into laughter."
Norman Wymer, from "The Inventors".

"On the highways it was
common to find groups of
sightless people ... drifting
wretchedly and hopelessly
from place to place, often
harried, usually ignored,
generally avoided or
repulsed for their ungainly,
shuffling gait, their ragged
dirty appearance, their
talon-like hands held out in
endless cadging and
pleading for scraps of food
... these people were
regarded as incomplete
beings, ignorant and
simple."

Lennard Bickel, from
"Triumph over darkness,
the life of Louis Braille".

could, so it was usually impossible to learn a trade or do work of any kind, and how else could a person expect to earn a living? Most blind people would have to depend entirely on others for everything they needed: they would be cared for if their family was rich and made provision for them, but if their family was poor or cast them out, they had nothing. Many had to beg on the streets for money and food.

And because blind people were so often helpless and uneducated, sighted people often interpreted their blindness as stupidity, treating them as outcasts, mentally backward and good for nothing except, at best, to be housed in an asylum out of harm's way.

So what was to become of Louis? As long as there were members of his family to care for him, he could want for neither love, food, clothing nor shelter ... but there must be more to life for him than this! The good Abbé Palluy was determined that no effort should be spared to find some way of settling young Louis on a more fruitful path, and he began making energetic enquiries of everyone he knew.

A special school in Paris

There are several different stories told about how Louis' family came to hear of the special school for the blind in Paris, but it seems most probable that the young teacher Bécheret remembered having heard of it, and that the Abbé Palluy, spurred on by this discovery, set out to discover more.

We know that he decided to approach the lord of the manor up in the grand chateau. The Marquis d'Orvilliers was a nobleman who had several times helped particular people in need in the village, and the priest had hopes of being given a sympathetic hearing.

He was not disappointed. The Marquis had noticed Louis in church on Sundays and listened with interest to the Abbé Palluy's plea for help in the matter of Louis Braille's future.

It turned out also that the Marquis himself knew of the school for the blind in Paris. He remembered that he had once met the founder, a gentleman by the name of Valentin Haüy.

It had been at the Royal Court of Versailles during the Christmas celebrations in 1786. Valentin Haüy had astonished the King and Queen and a large audience of the nobility of France with a unique display by blind children of reading and arithmetic! Indeed the Marquis himself, much impressed, had joined the royal couple and many others in donating money to Valentin Haüy's new school for blind children.

Urged on by the determined Abbé Palluy, the Marquis d'Orvilliers wrote at once to the Director of the school in Paris, and asked him to allow Louis to become a pupil.

A reply was not long in coming. Dr Guillié, Director of the Royal Institution for Blind Children in Paris, informed him that the Board of the Institution had agreed to offer Louis a place, and were even able to offer a small scholarship, to help pay the fees.

Louis was expected to join the Institution at its premises in the Rue Saint-Victor on February 15, 1819, shortly after his tenth birthday.

The journey to Paris

The long-awaited day dawned misty and cold. The stage-coach from the nearby town of Meaux was to carry ten-year-old Louis the forty kilometres through a winter landscape to Paris.

He had looked forward to this day. Yet now it was here, he was chattering in such a confusion of excitement and nerves, soaring hopes and plunging anxieties. Would it be like he wanted it to be? So far away! Would he be able to learn? Would he make new friends? Would it be difficult to find his way around?

His father was also talking a lot, describing the scenes passing by outside the coach so that Louis could share them. He, too, was deeply worried. He kept reassuring himself that it must be for the best to have his son go somewhere where he could learn things ... But it seemed so far from home. He was still so young ... Yet, if he could at least

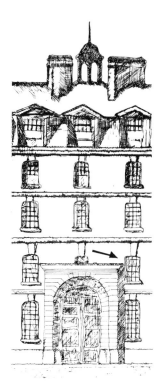

The Royal Institute for Blind Children in a damp, destitute area of Paris. When Louis arrived, he must have been bewildered and confused by the jostling crowds, the noise, and the overwhelming putrid stench of the nearby river mud, so different from Coupvray.

learn a trade: the school taught several, shoe-making, basket-weaving, rope-making, spinning and weaving, slipper-making, chair-mending ...

But what a gigantic city to leave him alone in! Even he, the adult and sighted Simon-René, found Paris strange and frightening, so large, so noisy, so full of strangers ... so different from the unhurried life of Coupvray.

Four hours of jolting and rumbling and worrying and speculating went by. Louis and his father entered the outskirts of Paris, and climbed down from the coach. From here on they would have to find their way on foot to the Latin Quarter. Somewhere close by was Rue Saint-Victor (St. Victor Street), and number 68, the building which was to become Louis' home, though they did not know it, for the rest of his life.

In 1819 the short journey to Paris took four hours by horse-drawn stage-coach through villages that Louis would never see. A century after his death his body would travel the same route from Coupvray, accompanied by representatives from forty nations, to its final burial amongst the great men and women of France in the Panthéon in Paris.

68 Rue Saint-Victor

It was not an attractive sight, that building in Rue Saint-Victor: official reports of the time tell us that the house was "in a low-lying district which is airless, evil-smelling and conducive to the spread of disease". It was dark and damp, a rabbit-warren of worn stairways and cramped corridors which must have filled Simon-René with apprehension. Where was the fresh brightness of Coupvray, the clear air and energetic outdoor life that Louis was used to leading?

But the meeting with the Director, Dr. Guillié, set his father's mind at rest. The boy would be well cared for, and there *was* a great deal he would learn here. In no time, he would be back for his holidays. And Louis, though nervousness was beginning to cloud his mind, was so insistent that this was what he really wanted to do.

A brief, close hug, many reassurances, and Simon-René left. Now Louis was truly alone. Strangers he could not see surrounded him, in a building he did not know, for the first time in his life.

Unfamiliar surroundings

He was taken straight to a class. The teacher's name was Monsieur Dufau, he was told by the Director. Nervously, Louis entered. The sound of shuffling feet told him that the pupils had got to their feet. There was a rustling as they turned to the door, then an abrupt order from Dr. Guillié that they should concentrate on their lessons.

Louis felt himself led by the teacher to a seat and without further ado the lesson resumed. It was geography, the course of the great River Seine through France. Within minutes nervousness, worries and shyness had flown. Louis knew nothing any more but those words of the teacher: every syllable he absorbed with a fascinated attention, and at the end of the lesson, much to the teacher's surprise, he could answer all questions without the slightest hesitation.

But after the lesson the strangeness swooped in on him again. What did the ringing bells mean?

"There were sixty pupils, and the headmaster treated them with great severity, punishing the boys for the most trivial offences by depriving them of their meals or sending them into solitary confinement."
Norman Wymer, from
"The Inventors".

23

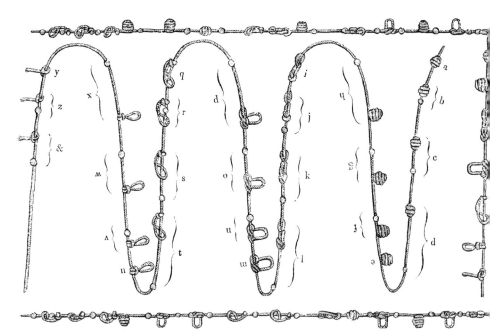

Over the centuries, in different countries, there had been the occasional attempt by a scholar to find a way of communicating the alphabet to the blind: one of the most intriguing was this method of conveying letters by knots on a string. Other scholars had attempted various forms of raised letters, carved in wood, in wax, and even one based on raised geometric shapes.

Where were all the feet going? The teacher introduced him to the other pupils, and he tried to memorize their names and their voices. But it was all just a mass of new smells and more bells, and hurrying feet that seemed to know exactly where they were going, while he stood in miserable confusion till someone took his arm and led him on.

Later, after he had unpacked his few belongings and put them beneath his bed, there was the silence of the dormitory, and the feel of other, unseen strangers in their iron beds, just like his.

New horizons

But at some stage in these first few days he made a friend, Gabriel Gauthier, who was to remain Louis' closest friend for the rest of his life. Gauthier had been at the school for some time, though he was only a year older than Louis. He knew his way around the endless corridors and twisting stairs, he understood the routine of life here, and so slowly, in his company, Louis learned, too, as they moved from room to room, from lesson to lesson, from meal to dormitory together.

There were also letters from Coupvray to help him through the early weeks, read to him by one of the supervisors at the school. The newness faded and the surroundings became familiar, part of his own territory. Now he could find his own way around, knowing, without counting, when he had moved enough paces along the corridor to the stairs, knowing how far from the dormitory door to his bed, from the classrooms to the courtyard and the dining room. He learned to recognize the voices of the boys and teachers.

And above all there were the lessons. Geography, history, arithmetic, grammar – he plunged into them with enthusiasm, showing all the promise that Abbé Palluy had been certain was there. The teachers spoke to the pupils and they repeated what they heard. And wonder of wonders, there were even some books, specially prepared for them. Louis was actually learning to read.

Just as the blind themselves were often caricatured, so was the idea of education for them: even in this drawing, the large, clumsy book seems to suggest something ridiculous. Valentin Haüy's books for the blind were as large as this – and could only be contained in several volumes!

Haüy's books for the blind

Valentin Haüy, founder of the school, had developed a way of printing books for the blind. Heavy paper was pressed onto a special, large lead type to make embossed letters – that is, letters raised above the surface of the page, which could be felt by the fingers.

There weren't many of these books in the school, as they were difficult and slow to make. Each letter had to be individually put in position, each piece of dampened paper put in the press and imprinted. It took weeks to make several copies of a single page, and it was not surprising that over the years, Valentin Haüy had succeeded in producing only a handful of books and pamphlets.

Big and clumsy the books were, each page made up of two pieces of paper pasted together, so that the raised letters on each side faced outwards. There were several religious texts and some grammar books in different languages – a rather strange collection to make up the basic library of the sixty or so children who were the pupils at the Royal Institution for Blind Children. But they were nevertheless books!

"The blind children could not learn their lessons from books. A few books had been printed in large raised letters so that the children could feel their shape, but, as each letter was three millimetres tall, they took up so much space that the children often forgot the beginning of a sentence before they fingered their way to the end."
Norman Wymer, from
"The Inventors".

Louis had to admit, though, that after the excitement when he first felt those raised letters under his fingers, there was a growing frustration. Reading was so slow. Each letter had to be traced with the fingertips, and then you had to remember it while you went on to the next one, and remember all of them in sequence until your fingers had passed the length of the whole word. It was all too easy to forget the first letters by the time you reached the end. And though Louis made good progress, it *was* difficult to feel the forms of letter.

A talented pupil

Louis' craft lessons posed no problems: basket-weaving, knitting, slipper-making, he enjoyed them all. At the end of his first year, he won prizes in these last two, showing again the nimble accuracy of his fingers that his family had discovered in the tasks they set him at home.

And there was music! The flute, the bassoon, the piano, all were taught at the school by music teachers who came specially from the Paris Conservatory of Music. They taught by guiding the pupils' hands along the instrument until they had memorized the position of the notes and the sounds they should make.

From the beginning, Louis discovered a special pleasure in playing music. He learned the piano, and it quickly gave him a sense of freedom which flowed through his playing and marked him out, early on, as a player of potential skill, whose natural talent would grow.

A new director

At the beginning of Louis' third year at the school, 1821, there was a significant change. The Director, Dr. Guillié, was dismissed, and a new director appointed. The pupils knew nothing about the reasons for Dr. Guillié's removal, but they were not sorry to see him go. For all his work in the school, he had been a brusque, unapproachable man, who had run the school strictly, with many harsh rules and regulations.

Louis showed considerable talent at school; he did well in all subjects, but especially in music. His parents began to lose their fear that he would become a destitute beggar, once they could no longer care for him. At least they could now hope that he could earn money as a musician – like the blind bagpipe-player in this painting.

The new director, Dr. Pignier, was very different. He seems to have been a dedicated man with a very deep interest in the progress of the pupils in his care. We also know a great deal more about Louis because of Dr. Pignier, for he has left behind his own written memories of the young student, from his first encounters with him.

There was also much excitement in those early months of 1821, for the school was preparing to welcome its founder, Valentin Haüy.

The old man had not visited the school for many years. He had accepted the Czar Alexander I's invitation to go to Russia to organize a project for educating blind children there, and he had only returned to Paris in 1817, after eleven years away. Efforts to revisit the school he founded had been very saddening: Dr. Guillié had not made him at all welcome.

"Possessed of a lively intelligence, he [Louis Braille] soon came to the fore through the progress he made and the success he gained in his lessons. Whether literary or scientific, his essays were models of exact thinking, remarkable for their precision of thought and for the clarity and correct language in which it was expressed. He had a fertile imagination but it was always controlled by his reason."

Dr. Pignier, from *"Biographical notes on three former professors of the Institution for Blind Children".*

The fair at St. Ovid, in 1771 where Valentin Haüy saw blind people clowning to the shouts and jeers of the audience. The sight of human beings so degraded and so helpless before the cruel laughter of others shocked him profoundly. It set his feet on the path which led to the foundation of the world's first school for the blind.

Dr. Pignier and the rest of the staff were not so eager to deny recognition to the man who had struggled for seventeen years to establish the first school for the blind in the world.

But Valentin Haüy had done much more than simply offer education to the uneducated. He was the first to raise the call that the blind were the equals of all other people, and should have the same chances in life – to education, self-support and independence. And his call had not gone unheard. In Germany, Austria, Prussia, England, Russia, schools for the blind had begun, inspired by the one in Paris.

The founder's legacy

Haüy himself had only understood how vast the chasm was between the sighted and the blind when he had witnessed a group of blind musicians decked out in donkeys' ears and huge spectacles performing as clowns before a hooting crowd at the September fair of St. Ovid in 1771. The experience had shocked him to the core, and he had determined to do everything in his power to change this appalling state of affairs.

But what an enormous burden of prejudice he had to roll back before he was taken seriously. The assumption that blind people must be stupid was deep-rooted, and people were not easily convinced that there was much point in spending time or money on trying to teach the unteachable.

It had been difficult to find both finance for his venture and blind people who would agree to be taught. Thirteen years later, in 1784, he had taken his first pupil off the streets: a sixteen-year-old beggar named François Lesueur who daily haunted the porch of the Church of St. Germain. François had been blind since he was six weeks old, and as long as he could remember he had been begging for his living. Valentin Haüy offered him a home and his first lessons.

He started teaching François to read with movable wooden letters carved on thin tablets, which he arranged to form words. It worked, and he was able to show his pupil's skill with some pride to the

Royal Academy, the gathering of France's foremost scholars and scientists. François' prowess at reading caused a sensation.

A school for blind children

Valentin Haüy's dream had become a reality: the world had its first school for blind children, twenty-four pupils gathered in an old house in Paris. Then had come the display at the Court of Versailles which the Marquis d'Orvilliers had witnessed, and more donations had allowed the school to grow. In 1791, the school was finally made a state institution, by government decreee.

But state control had also, in the end, led to the school being merged, at Napoleon's orders, with a refuge for the elderly blind called the Hospital of Quinze-Vingts. A year later, Haüy had been sacked.

Though it had now regained its independence and was once more a proper school for children separated from the functions of hospital and shelter, the aged founder had never been allowed to visit the institution he had fought so hard to create.

Haüy visits the school

One of the first acts of the newly-appointed Dr. Pignier was to put this right. He at once issued a formal invitation to Valentin Haüy, now an old man in his seventies, to pay an official visit to the Institution. They would spare no effort. Decorations in the classrooms, displays of learning and handicrafts, followed by a musical party. It would be the highlight of the term.

Louis remembered that meeting with the old man all his life. Instantly, he sensed the great happiness flowing from this brave pioneer as he saw, at last, the evidence of the work he had done. Here they were, living proof, these children, playing music, reciting poetry, singing a song dedicated to him as thanks for opening a world to them which was denied to so many others afflicted with blindness.

What a difference from the beggars and the creatures exhibited at fairs, grotesque in their clownish costumes, who had first roused his sympathy!

New seeds of conviction and determination were

This statue of Valentin Haüy with François Lesueur now stands in the grounds of the modern National Institution for Blind Children in Paris. It commemorates that first act of compassion and imagination by Valentin Haüy, when he took blind Lesueur as his first pupil, and taught him to read.

A text printed in the large embossed letters developed by Valentin Haüy. These books were very large: each page consisted of two pieces of paper pasted together so that the raised letters faced outward. The letters had to be large enough for the fingertips to detect their shape, so only a very short section of text could be fitted onto each page. Some subjects needed as many as twenty volumes each weighing nine kilograms. Reading them was also very slow: the shape of each letter had to be individually traced with the fingertips.

sown in young Louis that day, as he sang with the others and with the others shook hands with Valentin Haüy. For these last few months had brought another discovery to Louis, which had fired his mind with fresh excitement, new ambitions.

Barbier's dots and dashes

Earlier that year, an artillery captain in King Louis XVIII's army named Charles Barbier had come to Dr. Pignier with an interesting proposition. He had invented a form of writing using only raised dots and dashes. He had developed it so that military orders could be passed between soldiers secretly at night, no matter how dark it was: he had called the system "night-writing".

But then he had seen a display at the Museum of Industry: blind pupils had been demonstrating their reading from Valentin Haüy's books, those large pages filled with big embossed letters. Captain Barbier had been struck by how slow the process of tracing each letter's outline was.

It had prompted him to do further work, modifying his night-writing so that it could be used by the blind. He had explained the system, which he had renamed Sonography, to Dr. Pignier. It did not use individual letters to spell out the words, but conveyed whole sounds by groups of dots and dashes.

Over the years there had been several inspired inventors knocking at the door of the institution but once tried by the pupils, their ideas had proved useless.

Admittedly, the use of dots was something new. Other systems had all been based on the alphabet used by sighted people, modified so that it could be *felt* instead of *seen*. This suggestion about dots and dashes was sufficiently different for Dr. Pignier to listen carefully and discuss the invention in some detail, and declare that it should be tried out on the pupils.

Captain Barbier had to smother his impatience and be content with a period of waiting, for Dr. Pignier insisted that the system be tried out on the blind pupils.

The first Louis and his friends knew of the captain's invention, was when Dr. Pignier summoned the whole school together a few days later. There was a good deal of speculation about the meeting. What could be so important as to call them all together? Sixty children shuffled anxiously, amid equally intrigued supervisors and teachers. Expecting, perhaps, some new changes to the school organization or staffing, they were quite unprepared for the lengthy and careful description of Captain Barbier's invention, and for the few embossed pages which Dr. Pignier passed round for them to feel.

Louis masters the system

Dots! Louis was transfixed. One can imagine the first tentative touches, murmurs of interest rippling among the pupils, the slow tracing of the dots, the exploration of different shapes, then slowly gathering excitement as they all realized how much easier it was to distinguish *these* shapes than those large, raised letters in the books they were used to.

There were excited exclamations: everyone had an opinion; some felt daunted by the idea of learning something new; it was a bit complicated: it was faster, felt others. And with this they could not just read, but write too.

All agreed that it must be properly tried out, and so Captain Charles Barbier was informed that his Sonography would be incorporated at the Institution as an "auxiliary method of teaching".

Louis and his fellow pupils were eager to learn the new writing. With Louis' quick intelligence and dexterous fingers, he quickly mastered the process of composing words out of sounds expressed in dots. He learned Barbier's chart containing all the combinations of dots, and became skilled with the apparatus that Barbier had developed for writing.

This equipment was simple but very ingenious: there was a ruler with seven shallow grooves in it running its full length. To "write", you placed the paper on this ruler. A clip fitted over the paper and slid along the ruler. In the sliding clip there were little windows through which the writer could place the dots precisely on the paper, locating them neatly in the ruler's grooves. Dots or dashes were made with the aid of a slim pointed instrument with a large round handle, called a stylus: you simply punched it down, pressing dots into the heavy paper, so that on the reverse side they could be felt as bumps. The writer moved from right to left along the paper, so that when it was turned over, it could be read from left to right.

Throughout that winter the pupils worked enthusiastically with Barbier's invention. They were fascinated by the idea of being able to write, of being able to do some real reading. Louis and Gauthier spent many extra hours writing sentences to each other and then reading them back.

Problems with Barbier's system

But the better Louis became at using Sonography, the more he had to admit there were appalling problems with it. For a start, you couldn't spell with it: it was only designed to represent words as a collection of sounds. You couldn't put in commas, or full-stops, or any kind of punctuation in your sentences, for Captain Barbier hadn't worked out any combination of dots for that. Nor could you put any accent on the words (which is an essential part of spelling in French) or write numbers, or do mathematics, or write music....

And there were so many dots for a single word. Each symbol might be as many as six dots deep, and a single syllable of a word might need as many as twenty dots! It was too many to feel with one finger, and so many in each group to have to remember.

Without doubt it was vastly better than the embossed letters of Valentin Haüy, but gradually they all agreed that there were far too many dots, and the dots didn't say enough.

Louis meets Captain Barbier

Louis tried some tentative improvements. His experiments seemed to work, and in some excitement he showed them to Dr. Pignier. The Director, rather impressed, suggested that he should talk to Captain Barbier, and the inventor, equally intrigued, visited the school again.

The precise details of the meeting between Louis and Barbier have not been recorded, but we do know that Barbier was taken aback to find that a boy of thirteen claimed to have solved problems which he had failed to solve. Though he did acknowledge the usefulness of Louis' small improvements, he remained unconvinced by the boy's insistence that more basic changes were needed to reduce the number of dots and that spelling and punctuation should be introduced.

For all his concern for the blind children for whom he had developed Sonography, the captain could not share Louis' belief that they needed such an elaborate system. What could the blind want other than a means of basic communication? Why should they want a full alphabet, punctuation, even mathematics and music, that this ambitious boy was suggesting?

B   D   G

J   V   Z

R   GN   LL

IEN   ION   IEU

Barbier's sonography: the dots referred to a grid of six lines across by six rows down, in which Barbier placed sounds. The dots indicated the position of each sound in this grid: you counted the number of dots in the first column to find out which row down, then those in the second column to find out which line across.

From this Louis took the idea of using raised dots. But his system, by contrast, was brilliantly economic, precise and simple. It offered a small grouping of dots under the reader's fingers.

33

He did not understand the yearning for something that would allow the blind to enter the world of literature and science fully, able to read and compose the most complex of thought and convey it to others on paper.

Louis experiments

Faced with the obstinacy of Captain Barbier, who insisted that his system was as good as it needed to be, Louis gave up trying to convince him. But he was certain the improvements could be made. With or without Barbier, he would experiment and simplify. He would find something that was right, that was manageable, that could do everything a writing and reading language should do, with all the flexibility of the alphabet of the sighted.

And so thirteen-year-old Louis set off on his quest. He worked in all the spare moments he could snatch from the busy day of lessons, taking it up again at night as soon as the dormitory fell quiet, resuming in the early hours of the morning, pouring over it on his long summer holiday in Coupvray, calculating, experimenting, revising, working on and on and on.

First, he must reduce the number of dots so that each symbol could be instantly felt beneath one fingertip. He must also eliminate any arrangement of dots or dashes that might be confused with another arrangement: each group of dots must be unmistakably different from any other.

There was a solution. He was certain. It was only a question of finding it.

The dawn of braille

By October, when the new school year began, Louis felt his alphabet was ready. He had found a way of forming all the letters of the alphabet, the accents, punctuation marks and mathematical signs using just *six* dots and some small horizontal dashes. The cluster of dots for each sign was now so small that there was no need to move your finger at all: you could feel the whole group at once.

Gauthier, when he heard, could not contain his

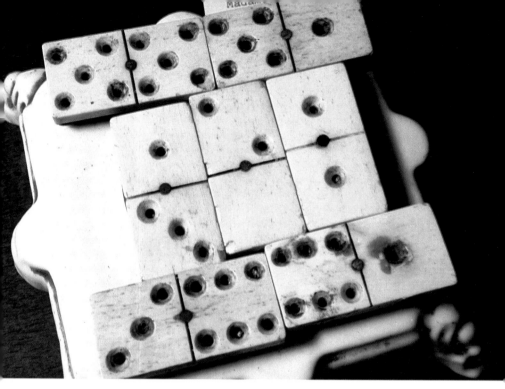

Above: Braille's personal dominoes: the dots have been removed to leave small dents which can be felt with the fingers.

Left: A Barbier ruler adapted for Louis' six-dot system is shown on the left, and on the right is an original Barbier ruler. They are lying on an early version of Braille's alphabet, which still included the dashes he later removed.

excitement. Groups of pupils gathered around as Louis wrote with dazzling speed and accuracy. Within hours the whole school knew, and Louis was summoned to Dr. Pignier to show what he had done. The Director watched the rapid demonstration with fascination: it was so simple, so accurate, and so clear. Just six dots: but the brilliant child had found a way of forming them into sixty-three combinations. There was truly something here!

There were still some details to solve, Louis assured him earnestly. Without hesitation, the Director congratulated the young pupil, and urged him to continue his experiments.

It took the other students little time to learn Louis' system. It held none of the frustrations they had experienced with Captain Barbier's dots. Dr. Pignier, impressed as much as anything with their tremendous enthusiasm for it and the unmistakable speed of their progress, had Barbier's rulers adapted for Louis' dots. The large "windows" in the sliding clip were divided into two smaller ones, so that each window allowed a maximum of six dots to be positioned within it.

For the first time, the pupils could take notes, copy passages they liked, even whole books, write letters to each other, keep diaries, write stories, all those things which a sighted person takes for granted and which had hitherto been out of reach.

For blind people, it was, unquestionably, the dawn of a new age.

Teacher and musician

His friends' excitement and enthusiasm was proof enough for Louis. He continued experimenting and perfecting his "little system," as he called it. But in all this time he never slackened off his other activities: his life continued as fully as before, occupied with his studies, in which he excelled, and his crafts, in which he also excelled.

In 1826, still only a student of seventeen, Louis began to teach algebra, grammar and geography to the younger pupils. Louis had found his vocation; this blind student was fast becoming an excellent teacher of the blind. It was a profession to which he

Below: St. Nicholas du Chardonnet, one of the churches near the Institution in Paris. Louis was able to express his talent as a musician and his deep religious faith, by working as organist at a number of churches. In them he would perform some of the first music ever translated into braille.

was perfectly suited, with his gentle manner, his lively gestures, his adaptable mind, and his liking and concern for his students.

Music continued to give Louis great pleasure. By now Louis was studying the organ, and in later years he became the organist at several churches of the city, a position which combined for the young man the chance to play music he loved, and the freedom to express his deep religious faith.

Coltat, his pupil and friend, tells us that his playing of the organ was "correct, brilliant, easy, typical of the whole tone of his personality".

The development of braille

Meanwhile we can trace the development and perfection of Louis' "little system", over a succession of years. First, in 1827 a grammar book was transcribed into his dotted alphabet, followed two years later by another grammar text. In 1828, he extended his system to the writing of music. By now he had removed the dashes from his alphabet. Practice had shown that although they were easy enough to feel, they were difficult to write well with the stylus.

By 1829, the first edition of Louis Braille's *Method of Writing Words, Music and Plain Songs*

"He never lost sight of this work. Never for an instant did he shirk the task of refining, developing and practising his new way of writing and reading."
Hippolyte Coltat,
Louis Braille's friend.

By 1828, Louis extended his system to the writing of music. On the left is the embossed music produced by Valentin Haüy, which had all the drawbacks of the large embossed letters. On the right is braille music of 1841. With this, blind musicians could not only read music, but also compose their own. Louis went on working on his system for many years, tirelessly experimenting, refining, polishing and improving.

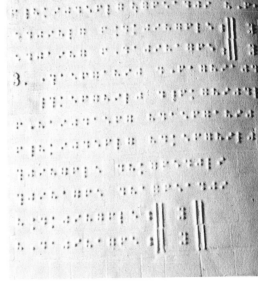

by Means of Dots, for use by the Blind and Arranged for Them, was published. This book was the formal birth of the original *braille* alphabet. But it would be many more years before it was officially adopted, even in Braille's own institution.

In his preface to this book, Louis Braille compared the improvements in his system with that of Captain Barbier. Yet he was scrupulously honest in giving Barbier full credit for the style of writing by dots. "We must say ...," he wrote, "that his method gave us the first idea of our own."

An inspired teacher

In August 1828, at the age of nineteen, Louis had officially become a teacher at the Institution, and when school began again after the summer holidays, he took on the teaching of grammar, geography, arithmetic and music.

As a teacher, Louis was a source of constant inspiration. "He carried out his duties with so much charm and wisdom," wrote his pupil Coltat, "that the obligation of attending his class was transformed into a real pleasure for his pupils. They competed not only to equal and surpass each other, but also in a touching and constant effort to please a teacher whom they admired as a superior and liked as a wise and well-informed friend, ready with sound advice."

Life continued for Louis the teacher in much the same way as it had for Louis the pupil. The rules seem very harsh at this distance of 150 years: he was unable to leave the school without permission, unable to receive visitors without permission, even his letters were read. And this was under the benign regime of Dr. Pignier!

But he no longer had to sleep in the dormitory: he had a room to himself. It was strange, at first, not to sense the others sleeping all around him, but then what luxury to have the peace and quiet to concentrate on his studies and research when the day's activities were over.

Louis was happy. His teaching absorbed him, his research absorbed him, and his friends absorbed

Opposite page: A teacher guides the hands of a blind child along a piano keyboard. Music has always opened new horizons for blind pupils, for it depended on a heightened sense of hearing and touch. Louis' friend Coltat has left us several descriptions of Louis as a teacher, gentle and kind, sharing the disability of blindness with his pupils, yet awakening in them the constant ambition to reach beyond their blindness into the outer world, always stimulating their minds with his wide-ranging knowledge, and caring for their progress in the utmost detail.

"The remarkable soundness of his mind, the correctness of his judgement and the acuteness of his intelligence, enabled him to foresee the sequence and consequences of events; as a result, there were few among us who knew him well who did not follow his advice and consider it excellent."

*Hippolyte Coltat,
Louis Braille's friend.*

him: he prepared his lessons using his own alphabet and began work on a book on arithmetic. His research on writing music progressed.

A time of loss

The year 1831, however, brought bad news: his brother, Louis-Simon, arrived to tell him that their father had died. To the end, Simon-René had worried about the fate of his blind son, still only twenty-two years of age. Louis-Simon brought with him their father's last letter, dictated on his death-bed, and addressed to Dr. Pignier. In it, Simon-René asked the Director never to abandon Louis, never to turn him out.

That evening Louis left for Coupvray, to be with his family in this time of grief, and to help his mother through the early days of loss. At least he was fulfilling his father's dearest wish: he had a profession and an income of his own. He could be a comfort to his mother; he would not be a burden, as too many blind people were.

Failing health

In these early years of the 1830s Louis was often un-well. By 1835 it was becoming impossible to ignore the increasing signs of some deep-seated illness. He was only in his early twenties, but he was always tired, frequently seized by fevers, and often troubled by a tightness in his chest.

One night he woke burning with fever, his mouth filling suddenly with blood. Desperately he called for help.

It did not take much for the school doctor to diag-nose what was wrong. Louis had suffered a sudden bout of internal bleeding. There could be no doubt that the young man was in the first stages of the dreaded tuberculosis, a disease of the lungs for which there was no cure.

At that time doctors knew very little about tuber-culosis, except to recognize the symptoms. They did not yet know that it was caused by a germ, carried in the close, damp air of places like the school and the dirty, crowded region of Paris in which it was situated. Clean, fresh air might have helped, but the only prescription the doctor could give was to rest more and eat well.

At once, Dr. Pignier arranged the teaching duties of his staff so that Louis need only have small classes; he would have to talk far less, and do little preparation.

Forced to reduce his teaching duties, Louis continued instead with his research. In 1836, he added the letter W to his alphabet at the request of an English pupil at the school. (The letter W does not appear in French.) A year later, he published a revised edition of the book on his system. He continued to call it his "little system of writing by means of dots", unaware that his name would one day be immortalized, when the "little system" became known world-wide as *braille*.

Raphigraphy

Now Louis became interested in how the blind and the sighted could write to each other. His raised dots were no use for this, because they relied on the sighted person learning *braille*. What was needed was for a blind person to write in a way already recognizable by the sighted – in the usual alphabet of the sighted – but be able to form the letters precisely.

By 1839 Louis had a solution. He developed a way of using the forms of the ordinary letters of the alphabet, maps, geometric figures, music, but made up out of raised dots: the blind could feel them: the sighted could instantly see them. Louis called this new invention Raphigraphy, and the students at the Institution seized on it as enthusiastically as they had taken up *braille*. Now they could write to their parents, and know their letters could be read.

The invention took another leap when Francois-Pierre Foucault, a creative and inventive blind friend of Louis' who lived at the Hospital des Quinze-Vingts, developed a machine for printing Raphigraphy. He attached type to levers which were

Below: Louis Braille's raphigraphy, a method of representing the letters of the ordinary alphabet with raised dots: this meant that both the blind and the sighted could read them; now a blind person could write to a sighted one.

Above: A braille globe of the world. Braille can be applied to any device requiring the use of the alphabet, numbers, music or scientific signs.

struck to imprint the letters on paper. It was no less than an early ancestor of the typewriter, and invented by a blind man!

The more his research developed, the more Louis perfected an extraordinary precision with words. So much space was needed to convey any word for the blind, even in his own system! The utmost economy was needed. And Louis was a genius at precision – this is why *braille* was to become the best system for blind people.

Opposition

Since 1829 Dr. Pignier had repeatedly asked that Braille's system be recognized as the official one at the school. In 1834 he had even arranged for Louis

Above: François Pierre Foucault, a blind inventor, developed this machine for printing Louis' raphigraphy. He called it a Piston Board.

Above left: The blind curator at the Valentin Haüy Museum in Paris operates a modern braille writer. By depressing the six keys in different combinations, the paper is embossed with the required braille signs.

to demonstrate *braille* at the Exhibition of Industry held in the great Place de La Concorde in Paris. And in 1837 the printing press of the Institution produced a three-volume history of France – the first book ever to be printed in *braille*.

But Dr. Pignier's requests for it to be fully recognized were not granted by the governing body of the school. Officially, the school must still use Valentin Haüy's embossed letters, cumbersome and inappropriate as they were, and of use only in printed form. Attempts over the years to teach writing of these letters had borne little fruit.

But to change the system would be expensive, for the books would have to be reprinted, the instruments replaced, and all the teaching methods at the school changed.

A bust of Louis Braille. His friend Coltat has left us a description of him: he was of medium height, with blond, curly hair; he always carried his head bent forward and tilted sideways in the characteristic pose which had been with him since childhood. He was relaxed in his manner, yet purposeful and agile in his movement, though the paleness of his face warned of his tragically frail health.

There were also many people who continued to believe that the system used by the blind must be one that was based on the same principles as the alphabet used by the sighted. To involve them in a special one, so the argument went, would create an impenetrable barrier between blind and sighted. This idea would persist in different forms for many decades, and was a major stumbling block to the acceptance of *braille* internationally.

Louis was much disappointed by the lack of support from the authorities and even wrote to the Ministry of the Interior himself. He got no reply. It was not until 1840, seventeen years after he'd first devised *braille*, that the first ray of hope was sent out from the officials, in reply to another of Dr. Pignier's renewed requests. This time, the answer was only that "This work strikes me as remarkable, and I think that Monsieur Braille ought to be encouraged." For all this, it was still Valentin Haüy's method that had to be taught officially to the children at the Institution.

Dr. Pignier is forced out

That year brought other severe disappointments. For some time, the vice principal of the school, Monsieur Dufau, had been trying to get rid of Dr. Pignier and gain control of the school himself. In 1840, with the help of one of the other teachers, he finally succeeded in persuading the authorities that Dr. Pignier was "corrupting the pupils' minds by his history teaching". Dr. Pignier was forced to retire early, and Monsieur Dufau was appointed in his place.

The school had lost the man who had for twenty years devoted himself utterly to the education and care of blind children, and they had lost their main champion of *braille*. Dr. Pignier had always allowed them to use it in the school, even though it was not officially recognized. From now on, it would be a very different matter. Monsieur Dufau was not renowned for his support of *braille*, and Louis and the other pupils feared problems in trying to continue with it.

The new principal

The years of 1840 and 1841 were altogether unhappy. In June of 1841, Louis' second sister, Marie-Céline, died in Coupvray. She was only forty-three and she left behind two young children, aged six and thirteen. The family's enormous sense of loss was made worse by their worry about Louis: he was constantly ill.

And the school under Monsieur Dufau was not pleasant: he wanted to establish his authority without question. He seemed to want to change everything. Each day brought something new, introduced at great speed, regardless of how distressing the pupils might find the rapid transformation from things they were used to.

Monsieur Dufau was also one of those who believed firmly that the blind should use the same alphabet as the sighted. Using a special one would separate them, he argued, close them off from normal intellectual life. He held firmly to these views despite the flagrant disproof provided by the students' preference for *braille* against the embossed alphabet.

Louis' health worsens

All the time Louis' health was worsening. He lost even more weight. And in the first months of 1843 he had more internal bleeding and began to cough blood again. He was forced to take to his bed for weeks at a time. Dr. Allibert, the school's doctor, was adamant that he needed far more rest and that he must give up his teaching. Louis and Monsieur Dufau agreed.

The weeks went by: visits from Louis' friends kept him up-to-date on even the smallest incidents in the school. Warmer weather seemed to bring an improvement in his health, and he began going out with Gauthier and Coltat to visit Dr. Pignier, who lived nearby since his forced retirement from the school. But on his return from one of these walks, Louis suffered further heavy internal bleeding. Now Dr. Allibert feared the worst. He insisted that Louis must go home to the country to rest.

"With him [Louis Braille] friendship was a conscientious duty as well as a tender sentiment. He would have sacrificed everything to it – his time, his health and his possessions. ... He wanted the objects of his friendship to profit from it. Thus he was watchful of their conduct, and often inspired them with firm and thoughtful advice. If the others showed understandable hesitation or reluctance to give what he considered important though painful advice to a mutual friend, he would laugh and say, 'Come, I'll sacrifice myself'."
Hippolyte Coltat,
Louis Braille's friend.

Home to Coupvray

So it was that the spring of 1843 found Louis in
Coupvray and there he stayed for six months. Fresh
air, his mother's cooking and care, the absence of
worries and release from the unpleasant atmos-
phere of rivalry and intrigue generated by Monsieur
Dufau at the school, seemed to help. He began to
feel a lot better. Yet Coupvray, too, held some sor-
row for Louis that year. Antoine Bécheret died. He
was the last of that trio of people who had been
so important in Louis' early life, for the Abbé Palluy
and the Marquis d'Orvilliers were already dead.

But there was great pleasure for Louis in the
company of the young members of the family, his
sisters' children. He had a particular bond of
companionship with eight-year-old Céline-Louise,
his dead sister's youngest daughter. Long hours
were spent walking and talking with her.

Back to Paris

Louis returned to Paris in October 1843, much re-freshed, only to find that things were a lot worse at the school. Monsieur Dufau had been influenced by the example of teachers of the blind in Scotland and the U.S.A.: he was changing the size of Valentin Haüy's embossed letters, and had burned all the old books, printed in the embossed alphabet!

All twenty-six printed by Dr. Guillié and the forty-seven printed by Dr. Pignier had gone up in flames. Now the blind pupils would have to learn to read all over again, getting used to completely new sizes and shapes!

Louis' dot alphabet was, needless to say, not included in Dufau's teaching plans, except for the writing of music notes.

But the pupils clung obstinately to *braille*. They taught each other outside the official classes and

The Braille family house in Coupvray as it is now: since the centenary year of Louis Braille's death, 1952, the house and his father's workshop have been preserved as a museum.

47

Blind guests arriving for tea. This shows a very different situation from the one depicted on page 18, though it shows again "the blind leading the blind". When the pupils at Louis' institute went out, they would walk in a line, joined by a rope. Louis Braille once said, "We do not want to be shut away from the world because we cannot see, and so we must work and study to be equal with others, not to be despised as ignorant or objects of pity. I will do all in my power to help you attain dignity through knowledge."

used it for all their own notes and correspondence, refusing to let go. Realizing the strength of their attachment, Dufau now openly opposed it, forbidding them to use it.

Help came from an unexpected quarter, from a friend of Monsieur Dufau himself – Joseph Guadet, his own new deputy. But Joseph Guadet, despite his friendship with the forceful Monsieur Dufau, was a man who judged for himself. He could not ignore the evidence of his own eyes: the blind pupils were so determinedly attached to Louis' system and insisted it was better than anything else. And how fast they could work with it! By comparison the progress made with Haüy's letters, even in the new sizes, was pitifully slow.

Guadet quickly became enthusiastic about Louis' alphabet, and set his mind to persuading the

obstinate Monsieur Dufau of its merits. It would not isolate blind people. Many *more* books could be transcribed in *braille* than in Valentin Haüy's embossed letters. What better access to science and the arts, to education, than a great many more books for them to read?

A new school

Among the stream of famous visitors, who at one time or another paid a call on the now famous school for the blind in Paris, was a well-known poet and historian, Alphonse Marie Louis de Lamartine. He had entered politics and become a Deputy in the Chamber of Deputies, and in 1838, he had spoken with conviction about the appalling living conditions in the Rue Saint-Victor. The Chamber of Deputies had been deeply moved by his description, and had swiftly voted enough money to buy some land in the Boulevard des Invalides and to build a new school there.

By November of 1843, the new building was ready. It must have been with a strange mixture of emotions that the pupils of Rue Saint-Victor packed up and moved: the ramshackle, insanitary old building had been home to many of them for years. But how spacious, clean, and airy the new buildings were. And perhaps Louis Braille might never have contracted tuberculosis had his life been spent in such surroundings.

"Yesterday I visited the Royal Institution for Blind Children. No description could give you a true idea of this building, which is small, dirty and gloomy; of those passages partitioned off to form boxes dignified by the name of workshops or classrooms, of those many tortuous, worm-eaten staircases, which, far from seeming suited to unfortunates who can guide themselves only by their sense of touch, are, if you will permit the expression, more like a challenge flung down to these children's blindness."

Alphonse de Lamartine
in his speech to the
Chamber of Deputies.

Approval for Louis' system

The official opening of the new school premises was on February 22, 1844. A large and distinguished audience, including members of the government, gathered for the ceremony, unaware they were about to witness another, momentous event. The school choir sang a song as a tribute to Valentin Haüy, composed by Monsieur Dufau and Gauthier. Pupils recited poetry and played music. Then it was Monsieur Guadet's turn to make a speech.

To Louis' amazement came the announcement that Dufau was going to describe the system of writing in raised dots. He proceeded to tell the

In 1843 the Institution for Blind Children moved to new buildings in a lighter, cleaner, airier part of Paris, on the Boulevard des Invalides. Les Invalides and the elegant gardens, shown in this picture, is at the northern end of this great boulevard. Louis spent his remaining eight years of life in the new premises, but it was too late for any recovery from tuberculosis.

audience about the problems with Captain Barbier's Sonography, and then the enormous advantages of Louis' system. He paid full tribute to the young inventor, seated in their midst. In no uncertain terms, Monsieur Dufau had forced the public to hear of *braille,* and an announcement, to such a gathering, accompanied by the publication of a pamphlet on the subject, was no less than an official approval of the forbidden dots!

The persistence and devotion of the blind pupils to the system of dots they knew was theirs, had triumphed. After twenty years of determination, Louis Braille's tremendous invention was finally, officially, acknowledged.

When the speech was over, Monsieur Guadet supervised a few experiments before the intrigued audience. One of the blind girls wrote down some poetry dictated by a member of the audience.

Another girl, who had not been in the room during the dictation, now entered and proceeded to read the writing perfectly. Then Monsieur Guadet had one of the teachers write down a musical phrase, dictated by one of the audience. Another blind pupil entered the room and read it back, again perfectly. And all so fast, so easily executed ...

There was thunderous applause. Braille knew an enormous happiness. Surely the continual battle for his system to be adopted, must be over.

Dufau makes amends

It certainly seems that Monsieur Dufau was, in the course of time, completely won over. In the years that followed he seems to have tried to make amends: over the years he worked very hard for permission to care for Louis as his illness worsened,

*"... the fact emerges that braille **was not established through the influence of interested parties, but by an urge from within, by the enthusiasm of those who, using it themselves, had daily experience of its worth; and by the recognition on the part of the seeing persons charged with the education of the blind, of the obvious progress accomplished by its adoption."***

Pierre Henri, from "The life and work of Louis Braille".

51

1848, the year of revolutions in France and Europe, caught Louis and his friends in its excitement. In Paris, workers and students threw up barricades, and with the soldiers of the national guard, declared a republic. Gauthier, Louis and others eagerly followed the republican movement whose beliefs they supported. Such a whirlwind of political upheaval would once have passed them by. Now, because of the gates which Louis' dots opened to them, they argued vehemently about the newspaper reports, wrote passionately and behaved like everyone else in these turbulent months.

at the Institution. For, despite the happiness of the opening ceremony, a combination of fatigue, excitement of the move, taking up his classes again, were all taking an intolerable toll on Louis Braille's health.

Within months, Monsieur Dufau relieved him of all duties at the school, and asked permission to keep him at the Institution to give him the care he needed.

Louis occupied himself with writing letters to his former pupils, obtaining, (at his own expense), books or writing instruments for them, asking them to copy books and paying them from his own money, then giving the books to others who needed them.

His friends tell us of many acts of kindness performed by this modest, gentle man, who never seemed to want to be thanked. He did these things because he felt they were needed and wished to do them, not because he wanted people to notice them. He even gave up his job as organist in one of the Paris churches to a colleague who had no work.

Three happy years

Louis survived the bad attack of tuberculosis that year, and the long rest seemed to be helping. By 1847, Dr. Allibert seemed to think he could start teaching again, and Monsieur Dufau allowed him to do so.

A teacher again! And even if he was short of energy, his chest delicate, and he was easily exhausted, it was nevertheless a three-year period of happiness; he conducted his lessons with zest and imagination, continued turning his creative energies to the problem of using *braille* to write music, and made short visits to see his family in Coupvray.

As early as 1847, new printing methods adapted to *braille* were tried out at the school. In all spheres of teaching, *braille* was beginning to show its qualities, such were the leaps in achievement by those who used it.

Louis' last years

By 1850 Louis felt that his strength was finally leaving him. He asked to be allowed to retire from teaching. Instead the Director offered to keep him on at the Institution and employ him for a few, very infrequent piano lessons.

By December of 1851 Louis knew he was dying. He was not yet forty-three years old. Coltat tells us of severe internal bleeding on the night of December 4.

Louis Braille lay dying, while outside barricades were thrown up on the streets of Paris and there was fighting on the boulevards.

More internal bleeding confined Louis Braille to his bed for what little was left of his life. In that calm, methodical and thoughtful way in which he had conducted his whole life, he put his affairs in order, arranging that his mother should receive a regular income from his savings, that the children of his brother and sisters should receive the rest of his property. His belongings at the Institution he left to Coltat, who distributed them as mementos to Louis' pupils.

"Despite his blindness, despite continual ill-health, despite the ill-will of others which delayed the recognition of his work, in the face of adversity and of accumulated disappointment he remained kindly, cheerful and faithful to his friends and to his ideal."
Jean Roblin, from his biography, "Louis Braille".

"Louis Braille was the apostle of light. If it is true that above all posterity remembers the work of a man extraordinarily persevering and methodical, with a prodigious power of concentration, we must yet recognize that not only did he have the mind of an inventor but also the soul of a saint."
Jean Roblin, from his biography, "The Reading Fingers, the life of Louis Braille, 1809-1852".

Louis died on January 6, 1852, two days after his forty-third birthday, much loved and much missed not only by those who had known him well and had felt the benefit of his honest, loving, intelligent nature for many years, but also by many who had been so strongly influenced and helped by this kindly, caring teacher.

Louis was buried at Coupvray. His body was taken back along the same route that he had travelled thirty-two years earlier when he had made his first journey to the Institution where he would achieve his life's work.

But the recognition of Louis Braille's work was still to come. Within the next three decades, he would become famed throughout the world as the greatest benefactor of the blind, the man whose work was the path by which millions of blind people would enter a new life because they could read, write, communicate, learn and create, and take their rightful place in society as cultured and educated human beings.

Braille spreads beyond France

Two years later, in 1854, *braille* was formally adopted as the official system for the blind in France.

Then it began to spread outside France. But it was a slow process, the task of convincing the teachers of the blind to abandon their belief in the need for methods based on the alphabet of sighted people. First in French-speaking Switzerland, *braille* began to be taught in the 1850s, and in 1860 the Swiss school for the blind at Lausanne printed the first book in *braille* outside France. German-speaking countries, by contrast, would take forty years before they adopted Louis' dot system.

In England the process was particularly slow. There were many systems of printing developed for the blind – in the ten years following Louis' basic work on *braille* there seems to have been at least twenty methods being tried. With few exceptions, they were based on some variation of embossed letters of the ordinary alphabet.

But *braille* found its champion: Dr. Thomas

Left: Louis' own watch: the glass can be lifted to feel the hands.

Above: A <u>braille</u> watch, using Louis' six-dot code.

Armitage, founder of the British and Foreign Association for Promoting the Education of the Blind, became very worried by the lack of order in teaching practice and printing: whatever system a blind person mastered, they were limited to working only with that system, and material produced in another system was incomprehensible to them. The various methods other than *braille* were also only ways of printing and reading: an individual could not write with them.

Dr. Armitage became committed to establishing a standardized system used by all the schools, and he was adamant that the blind were the only people qualified to decide which it should be. He set up a committee of blind people to assess the various methods available and select the best. They chose *braille*. By 1883 the great majority of British schools for the blind had adopted it.

International recognition

In 1878, there was a major step forward. An international congress of European nations – Austria, Hungary, Belgium, Denmark, Britain, France,

After the worldwide acceptance of braille in 1878, machines were developed for writing braille. Here a man is writing with Mauler's braille machine.

Below: Pupils using a braille globe.

Germany, Holland, Italy, Sweden and Switzerland – was held in Paris. It had assessed the various methods of printing and writing so as to establish a single, unified system world-wide. By a large majority, it voted for braille.

Now only the United States among the European-language-speaking countries continued to work with a multitude of systems, including forms of embossed alphabet, original braille and several forms of heavily modified braille. It took almost another forty years before only classic, original braille was taught!

By 1929 an international braille musical notation had been worked out; this would have delighted Louis Braille who had spent so many years working to extend his dots to music.

In 1932, a revised form of British braille was accepted by delegates from nearly a hundred nations. Within a short time it would be possible for almost any English-speaking blind person to write to any other, read any braille-printed book, newspaper or magazine.

Nowadays, braille has been extended to Indian dialects, Arabic languages, Japanese, Indo-Chinese language, Chinese, and a number of African dialects.

Modern technology

When the first book ever printed in braille was produced on the printing press at the Institution, (the short history of France printed in 1837), only one kind of type was made for it, containing all six dots. The pupils and tutors themselves chiselled off the dots not needed for each of the individual letters, so making the different types for the a',s, b's and c's and so on. These were then assembled into words.

The books were large and thick, made up of pages stuck back to back, with the dots protruding outward in just the same way as pages of embossed Haüy type. It was altogether a long, slow process to put a manuscript into print. But already by 1849 there were experiments in printing by using stereotyping, that is, using whole sheets of metal containing all the embossed symbols for a page.

Today, it is possible to use both sides of the paper, and both sides of the printing plate, by what is called "inter-pointing" – a slight shift in the position of the dots on the second side, so that they do not coincide with the dots on the first.

Another major development was the invention of the braille writer, by Frank Hall in the U.S.A. This was a machine with six keys (one for each dot) operated by pressing several keys simultaneously to make all the dots in any one letter with a single action. Writing *braille* by hand, it is difficult to reach speeds of more than fifty or sixty letters a minute, but the braille writer allows twice that speed, with little tiredness. Typesetting machinery for printing was developed along the same lines, and models were shown at the Chicago Exhibition in 1893.

Braille in the computer age

In an effort to save space and increase the speed with which *braille* can be read and written, a wide variety of abbreviations and shortened forms of commonly occurring words have been developed, to supplement the original alphabet.

But the transcribing of books into *braille* has always needed a sighted person trained in *braille*. In the late 1950s computer-aided braille printing was developed in the U.S.A. For the first time, *braille* could be produced by someone not skilled in *braille*. A typist using an ordinary keyboard puts the manuscript onto the computer. The computer program then transcribes it into *braille*. These machines are now aided by modern word-processing facilities, vastly improving the ease, speed and accuracy with which manuscripts can be set, altered and corrected on the computer before the metal printing plates are embossed.

More recently machines have been developed which can electronically "read" an ink-print text into the computer-aided braille-production system four times faster than someone typing it in at a keyboard, and without any human typing error.

The development of personal computers has

Moon, a system developed by Dr. William Moon. It is the only one of the systems competing with braille *in the 1860s which still survives. These days it is used by some people blinded in middle or later years. Because they are already accustomed to the ordinary alphabet, they find it easier to use a system like Moon which is based on a modified, simplified alphabet, rather than to learn a completely new system.*

"Today the best books by modern authors – as well as newspapers and magazines – are published in braille in nearly every country in the world. In Britain alone as many as 50,000 books and half a million periodicals may be printed in a single year."
Norman Wymer, from *"The Inventors".*

Above: A South African reading a braille *Bible. Right: A blind Nigerian girl is shown a* braille *tape-measure. According to the Helen Keller International Report for spring of 1987, there are forty-two million blind people in the world.* Braille *can be developed for any language using the Roman alphabet which does not have more than one accent per letter; it can also be developed for most non-Roman alphabets.*

"It is high time for Louis Braille's genius to be recognized throughout the earth and for the story to be told of the godlike courage and the heart of gold with which he built a large, firm stairway for millions of sense-crippled human beings to climb ..."

Helen Keller.

---

opened up enormous possibilities, not least machines and programs which allow a blind person to write, proofread and correct writing using a *braille* keyboard and *braille* display, yet obtain a printed copy not just in *braille* but also in ordinary ink-print alphabet.

One of France's heroes

A hundred years after Louis' death, the gift of that thirteen-year-old boy who devised the six-dot system was formally acknowledged as the invention of world-wide significance that the blind had long known it to be. In June of 1952, representatives from forty nations came to pay their respects to Louis Braille at his grave in Coupvray, and then accompanied his body on its last journey to Paris, to the Panthéon, to be buried among the great men and women of France.

One thing is certain: whether buried in the Panthéon or in his village of Coupvray, Louis Braille's name is unlikely ever to be forgotten. As long as there are blind people to use *braille* to share in the intellectual heritage of the world and live as equals alongside sighted people – educated and independent as Louis Braille dreamed they could be – his name will be remembered.

Left: Learning to use braille typewriters at a school for the blind. Some braille typewriters type letters in braille and others type in normal script. Speed is no longer a problem. When braille is written by hand a blind person can write at speeds of about ten words per minute, but machine braille writers with six keys can double this speed, while an experienced braille reader can accomplish speeds of around a hundred words a minute.

Left: Braille playing cards, with the numbers written in the six-dot code.

Important Dates

1771   Sept: Valentin Haüy sees blind people being mocked at a fair. He decides to start a school to help them.

1784   The Institut des Jeunes Aveugles, founded by Haüy, opens in Paris.

1786   A group of blind children from the Institute give a demonstration of finger reading at Versailles. Louis XVI gives the school the royal patronage.

1789   The French Revolution: Haüy is dismissed as principal of the school.

1800   On Napoleon's orders, the blind children are dumped in an asylum for handicapped people.

1806   Haüy flees the revolutionary fury with Remy Fournier, one of his students. They go to Prussia and start a school.

1807   As Napoleon's armies advance, Haüy and Fournier escape to Russia and set up another school for blind children.

1809   Jan 4: Louis Braille is born in Coupvray, France.

1812   Summer: Louis, aged three, blinds one eye in an accident.

1813-14   He gradually loses the sight of the other eye as well.

1814   Russian troops occupy Coupvray as Napoleon's empire falls. Captain Barbier starts work on his "Night-Writing" system.

1815   Jacques Palluy becomes the parish priest of Coupvray and starts teaching Louis. The Institut des Jeunes Aveugles reopens in Paris.

1816   Antoine Becheret offers Louis a place in the Coupvray school.

1819   Louis leaves for Paris to attend the school founded by Haüy. He is ten years old.

1821   Barbier demonstrates his "Night-Writing" to the Institute. The students are delighted. Dr. Pignier becomes the new Director.

1824   After two years' work, Louis completes his first "dot" alphabet, based on Barbier's invention. He is just fifteen.

1825   Louis learns the piano and shows great musical talent.

1827   A French grammar book is transcribed into Louis' six-dot system.

1828   Louis is appointed an assistant teacher at the Institute and he adapts his system to write down music.
The Institute building is condemned as unhealthy by a panel of doctors.

1829   Louis publishes a booklet explaining his six-dot system.

1833   Louis is appointed as an organist to a nearby school. He continues working as an organist for the rest of his life.

1834   The governors of the Institute refuse to allow the students to use Braille's dot alphabet. He demonstrates his system at the Exhibition of Industry in Paris.

1835   The first symptoms of tuberculosis appear in Louis.

1837   The first book in *braille* is written and printed at the Institute by blind teachers and students.

1838	May 14: Lamartine denounces conditions at the Institute in the National Assembly; 1,600,000 Francs are voted for a new building.
1839	Louis starts work with sighted helpers on machines to print *braille*. He develops Raphigraphy, using raised dots in the form of ordinary letters.
1840	Dr. Pignier, the director of the school, is forced to retire. His deputy, Dufau, takes over and destroys all previous books for the blind. He brings in new reading systems. Guadet becomes his deputy director.
1841	Francois-Pierre Foucault invents his machine for typing Raphigraphy.
1843	Louis' health fails; he goes to Coupvray for six months. Nov: The new school is finished and the move completed.
1844	Feb 22: The new school is officially opened and a totally convincing display of *braille* is given by the students.
1847	Foucault, in collaboration with Louis Braille, finishes his development of a *braille* typewriter.
1848	Louis' illness worsens; he can only give a few music lessons.
1851	Louis is so ill that he goes into the Institute's hospital.
1852	Jan 6: Louis dies, aged forty-three, and is buried in Coupvray.
1854	*Braille* is adopted as the official system for the blind in France.
1878	An International Congress chooses *braille* as the best system for the blind to be promoted world-wide.
1917	*Braille* is accepted for general use in the United States.
1929	International *braille* musical notation is adopted.
1949	India asks UNESCO to regulate *braille* for use in all languages. Over one hundred languages and hundreds of dialects can now be written in *braille*.
1952	Braille's body is removed from Coupvray and reburied in the Panthéon in Paris – the highest recognition for any French citizen.

Further Reading

Bickel, Leonard: *Triumph Over Darkness: The Life of Louis Braille* (Unwin Hyman), 1988
Christiaens, J.: *Conquerer of the Night* translated from French by Anthea Bell (London: Abelard and Schuman, 1970)
Hemry, John: *Braille Music: an international survey*, National Library for the Blind, 1984
National Library for the Blind: *Books in Braille*, published six times a year
Niemark, Anne E.: *Touch of Light: The Story of Louis Braille* (New York: Harcourt and Brace) 1970

Glossary

Abdicate: To resign as king or emperor and retire into private life.

Antibiotic: A chemical substance, such as *penicillin*, that can destroy or inhibit the growth of disease-causing micro-organisms.

Asylum: Literally a refuge or place of safety. So a place where people with problems can live sheltered from society.

Awl: A pointed tool with a fluted edge used for cutting holes in wood or leather.

Barricade: A barrier in the street, built with carts, furniture and anything else to hand. The Parisians were inclined to "go to the barricades" whenever they were dissatisfied with political affairs.

Bavaria: A kingdom in the south-west of Germany; now a state in the Federal *Republic* of [West] Germany.

Billet: To lodge soldiers in private houses, rather than having them camp out.

Bushel: A British measure of dry or liquid substances equalling 8 Imperial gallons or 36.4 litres.

Cavalry: Soldiers who are trained to fight on horseback.

Chamber of Deputies: The lower house of the French Parliament.

Chateau: A French country house or castle.

Congress: An international conference of experts and interested parties in a particular topic.

Coup d'etat: (from the French, meaning "stroke of state") A sudden, often violent, and illegal seizure of government.

Czar: (or Tzar) The Emperor of Russia.

Dominoes: A game played with counters with dots. It became very popular in Braille's childhood.

Dormitory: A room where three or more people sleep.

Germ: Any micro-organism that causes disease.

Grammar: The system of rules which organize the way a language works.

Inter-pointing: The system of off-setting *braille* printing so that the dots on the second side of the page do not coincide with those on the first side.

Napoleon Bonaparte: 1769-1821. Born in Corsica, he came to power in 1799 after a *coup d'etat*. A brilliant general, he conquered most of Europe between 1800 and 1813. He was finally defeated at the Battle of Waterloo (1815) and sent into exile on St. Helena in the south Atlantic.

Penicillin: An *antibiotic* made from a fungus and used to treat a wide variety of infections.

Prussia: A kingdom lying in modern north-eastern Germany and Poland, which became the dominant country in the German Federation. In 1871, the King of Prussia became Emperor (Kaiser) of Germany.

Raphigraphy: Braille's name for his method that allowed blind people to write letters that sighted people could read. In 1841, Francois-Pierre Foucault invented a machine for typing Raphigraphy.

Republic: A form of government in which the people, or their elected representatives, possess supreme power. The ruler of such a state is usually a President.

Saddler: A skilled craftsman who makes all types of harness for horses, but particularly saddles.

Scholarship: Financial aid provided for a student who shows outstanding academic ability.

Sonography: The "night-writing" developed by Captain Charles Barbier for military use. It inspired Braille to develop his own dot alphabet.

Stylus: A pointed tool for drawing on wax or engraving on metal. Used by Braille to prick his dots into paper.

Tuberculosis: An infectious disease caused by a *germ* which mainly attacks the lungs. It can be caught by drinking milk from infected cows, or from breathing in dust which contains the germs coughed out by other humans. These germs can live for weeks in dust and dirt under damp conditions. They are killed by sunlight. If people live in dark, dirty and badly-maintained buildings, like the old Institute, they are much more vulnerable to this disease.

Versailles: A palace built for Louis XIV and lying near Paris.

How YOU can help (tips from the RNIB)

● If you meet a blind person in the street who looks as if they might need help, ask them. If they would like you to guide them **don't** push them ahead of you – perhaps into a busy road – but **do** offer your arm, and let them follow you safely through the traffic.

● Let the blind person take your arm and walk slightly in front of them watching out carefully for obstacles.

● Stop at the top of the stairs or steps and say whether they are going up or down, and about how many there are. If there is a hand-rail, put the blind person's hand on it to help them. Say when you reach the bottom step.

● Help them to sit down by putting their hand on the back of the chair, and leave the rest up to them. Don't lower them bodily into a seat they have not inspected.

● If you need to walk in single file, indicate this by bringing your guiding arm behind your back.

● Don't leave hazards in their path. See that your hedge is cut back, your bike isn't left in the middle of the pavement, and your banana-skin is deposited where it belongs: in a rubbish bin.

● If you go up to a blind person to say hello, tell them who you are in case they don't recognize your voice. And when you are going to leave, tell them: it can be embarrassing for them to find themselves talking to an empty space.

● If you are visiting a blind person, don't move things around – it may take the person hours to find them again.

● Try doing some everyday activity like eating your lunch, making a drink, doing your hair or looking for something in your desk or wardrobe without using your eyes.

● Contact your local voluntary society for blind people, or your local social services department, and offer your services as a volunteer to visit an elderly blind person, do their shopping, go for a walk with them, or read to them.

● Remember that blind people are normal people who just can't see, and treat them as you'd treat anyone else – except at those times when they need a little extra help, just as you would in their place.

Useful Addresses

Australia
Welfare Association for the Blind
P.O. Box 181
Woollongabba
Queensland 4102

Braille Society for the Blind
61 Kitchener Avenue
Victoria Park
Western Australia 6100

New Zealand
Royal New Zealand Foundation for the Blind
Private Bay
Newmarket
Auckland

Britain
RNIB
224 Great Portland Street
London
W1N 6AA

London Association for the Blind
14/16 Verney Road
London
SE16 3DZ
(a national organization)

Index

Armitage, Dr. Thomas 54-5

Barbier, Captain Charles
30, 32, 34, 36, 39
develops sonography 30-1
first used at Royal
Institution 32
problems with 32-3
meets Braille 33
Bécheret, Antoine 17, 18,
20, 46
Braille 41, 42, 43, 44, 47, 53,
54, 55, 58
adopted in France 54
adopted in Britain 55
birth of alphabet 37-9
dawn of 34-6
demonstrated at Royal
Institution 49-51
development of 37
international recognition
55-6
mechanical writer for 57
modern technology and
56-8
musical notation 56
official recognition of 50
opposition to 42-4, 45,
47-8
spread of 54-5
revised form of 56
Braille, Louis
birth 9
burial at Panthéon 58
childhood in Coupvray
7-15
death 54
death of father 40
demonstrates *braille* 34-6
develops *braille* 5-6,
37-9
develops raphigraphy 41
family 7-8
friendship with
Gabriel Gauthier 24
friendship with
Abbé Palluy 17
ill health 40-1, 45, 51-3
legacy 58
loses sight 11-14
meets Captain Barbier
33-4
meets Valentin Haüy
29-30
musical interests 37
publication of book 37-8

receives approval for
system 49-51
recognition of work 54
and sonography 31-4
starts at Royal Institution
for Blind Children 21-5
starts school in Coupvray
18-19
teacher at Royal
Institution 36-7, 39-40

Coupvray 9, 17, 22, 23, 25,
40
occupation of 15-17

Dufau, Monsieur
becomes Director of
Royal Institution 44
opposes use of *braille* at
Royal Institution 45,
47-8

Fleming, Alexander 13
Foucault, Francois-Pierre 41

Gauthier, Gabriel 24, 32,
34, 45, 49
Guadet, Monsieur 48, 49,
50-1
supports use of *braille* at
Royal Institution 48-9
Guillié, Dr. 21, 23

Hall, Frank 57
Haüy, Valentin 21, 28, 49
books for the blind 25, 47,
49
decides to help blind
people 28
founds school for blind
children 28-9
sacked from Royal
Institution 29
visits Royal Institution
29-30

Inter-pointing 57, **62**

de Lamartine, Alphonse
Marie Louis 49

Palluy, Abbé Jacques 17, 20,
25, 46
and Braille's future 20-1
Pasteur, Louis 13
Pignier, Dr. 28, 36, 39, 40,
41, 45
becomes Director of
Royal Institution 29

champion of *braille* 42-3,
44
forced to retire from
Royal Institution 44
invites Valentin Haüy to
Royal Institution 29
and sonography 31

Raphigraphy 41-2
Royal Institution for Blind
Children 21, 25
Dufau becomes Director
of 44-5
offers place to Braille 21
Pignier becomes Director
of 29
premises of 22-3
moves to new building 49

Sonography 30-1, **62**
improvements to by
Braille 33-4
first used at Royal
Institution 32
problems with 32-3